A Chip in Tom's Ship

By Cameron Macintosh

T0360172

Tom went for a jog with Mum.

"They will have fun!"
said Sam.
"And I can have fun with
Tom's red ship!"

Sam got Tom's red ship
in the box.

Then Sam let it go!

The ship fell!

It hit Tom's bed.

Wham! Thud!

"Tom's ship has a big chip!" said Sam.

"What will Tom do when he sees it?"

"I have to fix it!" said Sam.

Sam got her kit.

She put lots of red
in the chip.

When Mum and Tom got in,
Tom was sad.

"My red ship is wet!"
said Tom.

"I let go of it," said Sam.
"It hit the bed, but I fixed it.
Do not be mad, Tom!"

Tom looked at the ship.

"I am not mad, Sam,"
said Tom.
"You fixed it well!"

CHECKING FOR MEANING

1. Where did Tom and Mum go? *(Literal)*

2. How did Tom's ship get a chip? *(Literal)*

3. Why did Sam wait until Tom was away from the house to play with the ship? *(Inferential)*

EXTENDING VOCABULARY

wham	What is the meaning of *wham*? Do you know any other words that have the same meaning? When the name of a word imitates the sound that it describes, it is called onomatopoeia.
chip	What would a *chip* in the ship look like? Have you ever chipped something? How did it happen?
then	What does the word *then* mean? Use it in a sentence to show it can mean *next* or *after that*.

MOVING BEYOND THE TEXT

1. Do you think Sam should have taken Tom's ship out of the box when he wasn't there? Why?

2. Have you ever played with a toy that wasn't yours and damaged it? What happened?

3. Did Sam do the right thing to fix Tom's ship? Why?

4. Do you think Tom was kind to Sam when he saw she had fixed the ship? Why?

SPEED SOUNDS

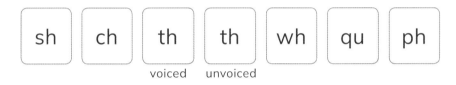

sh	ch	th	th	wh	qu	ph
		voiced	unvoiced			

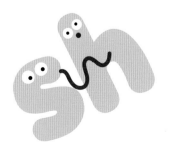

PRACTICE WORDS

Then

ship

Wham

chip

Thud

when

When